uper Dad, Pop, Daddy-O,

Dad, Papa, Father, Daddy,

, Dear Dad, World's Greatest Dad.

Super Dad, Pop, Daddy-O,

Dad, Papa, Father, Daddy,

O, Dear Dad, World's Greatest Dad

dy, Super Dad

To my dad, Jacques, my brothers, and all dads who,
whether far away or close, are always near in happy times.
—D. B.

Concept: Diane Barbara.
The authors would like to thank the following people for their help:
The documentation service of the Parents' School and all the children
who did such a good job of "putting on their thinking caps" about the topic of their fathers,
in particular the students of CM2 (2001) of Stanislas College.

Diane BARBARA and Serge BLOCH

Dad and Me

Harry N. Abrams, Inc., Publishers

Most of the time,
you think you know everything about your dad.
But getting to know him
is like exploring an island—the closer you look,
the more exciting things you will find.

This album is for you and your father to fill out, page by page.
Forget what you already know about each other
and get ready to discover many new and wonderful surprises!
Because you and your dad have a special story to tell.

A Dad Is Like a Captain

Some say that a dad
is like a captain of a ship.
He trains his crew,
watches over them,
and steers them
in the right direction.
He is always there
when the waves get rough,
and he guides them
safely through every storm.

Before I Was Born

Most dads are just as excited about parenthood as moms are. They can't wait for the big day! Here are some insights on what expecting a baby is like.

Hey, Dad, tell me . . .

How did you find out you were going to be a dad?

_____
_____
_____
_____
_____

What were you doing when you heard the news?

_____
_____
_____
_____
_____

Did you talk to me when I was in Mom's belly? Did you feel me kick?

_____
_____
_____
_____
_____

Were you hoping for a boy or a girl?

_____
_____
_____
_____
_____

Did you go with Mom to her doctors' appointments? Did you see me on the sonogram?

_____
_____
_____
_____
_____

Did you have to buy anything special before I arrived?

_____
_____
_____
_____
_____

When did you realize you were really a dad?
• When Mom's belly started to grow?
• When you saw me for the first time?
• When you held me in your arms?

If you and Mom adopted me, tell me the story of how you found me.

Glue a picture below of Mom when she was pregnant with you or the day you were adopted.

Date: Place:

The Big Day

_____ , my birthday

Where was I born? _____

What time of day was it? _____

What was the weather like? _____

Were you in the delivery room? _____

_____

_____

Who else was there? _____

What did Mom say when she first saw me? ___

_____

What did you say when you first saw me? ____

_____

How did you feel when you first held me? ____

_____

_____

If I was adopted, what was our first meeting like?

_____

_____

_____

_____

_____

_____

_____

How did you choose my name? _____

_____

If I had been born the opposite sex, what would my name have been? _____

Who filled out the birth certificate? _____

Who was the first person you told about my birth? _____

Where and when did my brothers and sisters see me for the first time? _____

_____

What were their reactions? _____

_____

Who was my first visitor? _____

What were my first days like? _____

_____

_____

My first baby picture!

Date: Place:

*Paste one of
your first baby
pictures here.*

*Hey, Dad,
how much older are
you than me?*

_____

What Kind of Dad . . .

Some dads are domestic. They love bottle-feeding, changing diapers, and making baby food. Some dads are active. They love going for walks or teaching you how to swim. Ask your dad the following questions to find out more about what kind of dad he is.

LET'S GO FOR A WALK!

Life's Firsts

	Yes	No		Yes	No
Did you change my diapers?			Did you push me in the stroller?		
Did you feed me?			Did you teach me how to walk?		
Did you bathe me?			Did you teach me how to talk?		
Did you read to me?			Did you teach me how to sing?		
Did you make meals for me?			Did you bring me to day care?		
Did you burp me?			Did you come with me to my first day of school?		
Did you cuddle me?					
Did you babysit me?			Did you teach me how to swim?		

Date:

Place:

Date:

Place:

Date:

Place:

Find photos of you and your dad doing some of the activities mentioned on page 10

Hey, Dad, when was the first time I called you "Dad"?

Hey, Dad, what story was your favorite to read to me?

11

A Chip Off the Old Block

Do you have your dad's nose?
What about his smile?
Do you both have dimples or freckles?

♥ Our Portraits

Do we look alike?

My Dad	**Me**

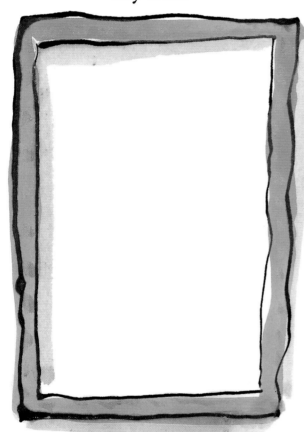

Date: Place:

Date: Place:

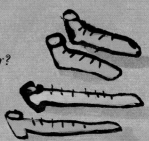

Take a picture of your dad.
Then let your dad take a picture of you.
Paste both of the photos above. Do you resemble each other?
If so, draw little arrows pointing out the similarities.
Do others in your family see what you see?

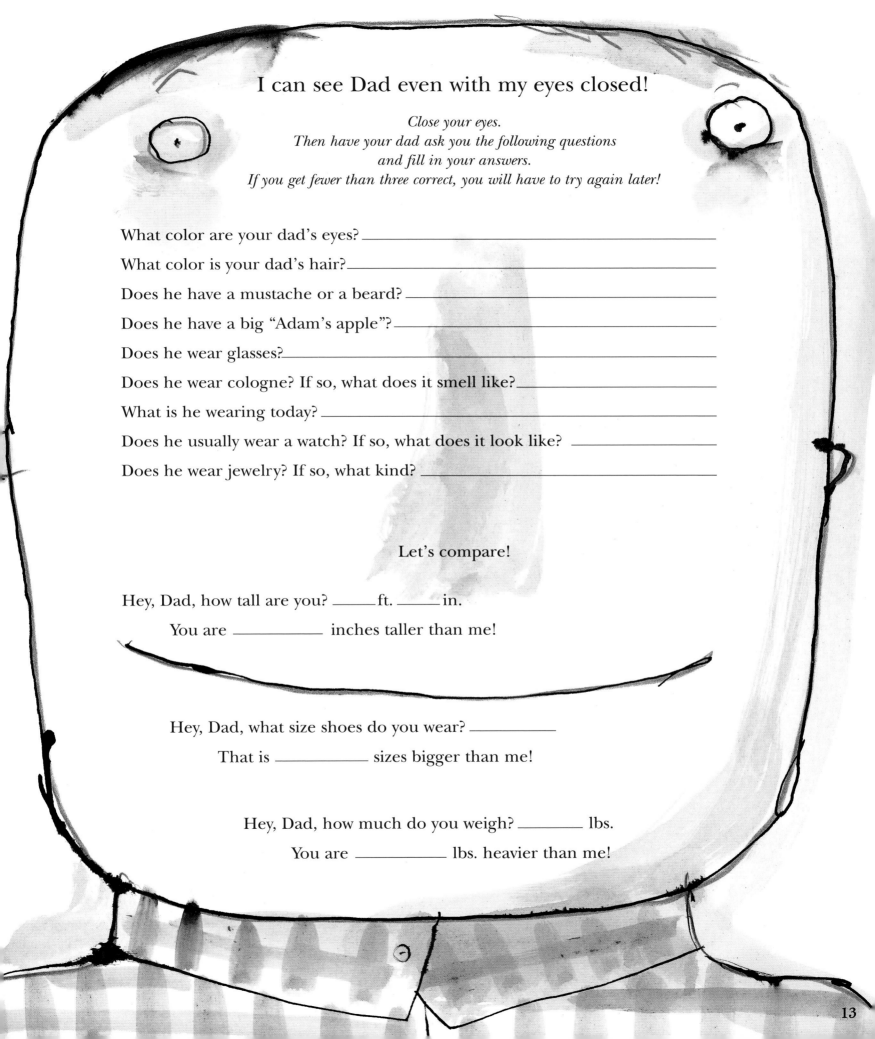

I can see Dad even with my eyes closed!

Close your eyes.
Then have your dad ask you the following questions
and fill in your answers.
If you get fewer than three correct, you will have to try again later!

What color are your dad's eyes? _____

What color is your dad's hair? _____

Does he have a mustache or a beard? _____

Does he have a big "Adam's apple"? _____

Does he wear glasses? _____

Does he wear cologne? If so, what does it smell like? _____

What is he wearing today? _____

Does he usually wear a watch? If so, what does it look like? _____

Does he wear jewelry? If so, what kind? _____

Let's compare!

Hey, Dad, how tall are you? _____ ft. _____ in.

You are _____ inches taller than me!

Hey, Dad, what size shoes do you wear? _____

That is _____ sizes bigger than me!

Hey, Dad, how much do you weigh? _____ lbs.

You are _____ lbs. heavier than me!

♥ Our Favorite Things

Everyone has their own taste. Your dad has his, too. Some of them you agree with; others you don't understand at all.

Who knows the other's tastes better? Which do you have in common?

Dad's tastes according to me	My tastes according to Dad
His favorite color _____	My favorite color _____
His favorite place _____	My favorite place _____
His favorite food _____	My favorite food _____
His favorite object _____	My favorite object _____
His favorite outfit _____	My favorite outfit _____
His favorite outfit of Mom's _____	My favorite outfit of Mom's _____
His favorite children's story _____	My favorite children's story _____
His favorite song _____	My favorite song _____
His favorite TV show _____	My favorite TV show _____
His favorite season _____	My favorite season _____
His favorite flower _____	My favorite flower _____

Respond to this small quiz on two separate pieces of paper.
Then copy both sets of answers onto this page
and go over the results together.
Show off your knowledge to the rest of the family!

♥ My Dad's Moods

My dad is happy when
_____
_____

Dad gets really upset if
_____
_____

Dad is quiet when _____
_____

My dad laughs like crazy at
_____

GRR GRR GRR GRR GRR GRR GRR

My dad is in a good mood when _____

He gets excited when you ask him to _____

And me, I get cranky when
_____

What Is a Dad Made Of?

Find nine words describing your dad that begin with these letters, such as "Devoted" for the letter D. It will be Dynamite!

D _____
A _____
D _____
D _____
Y _____
D _____
E _____
A _____
R _____

15

Special Moments

Sometimes when you are with your dad,
you have unforgettable moments
when you are both *so* happy
that everything in the world seems perfect.
These special moments
are as bright as the stars in the sky.
Each time you look at the stars
try to remember all of the reasons
you love your father so.

He tickles me

He is strong

He protects me

We laugh together

He teaches me
new things

He takes me o
to lunch

He takes me on
fishing trips

He takes me
to school

He plays outside
with me

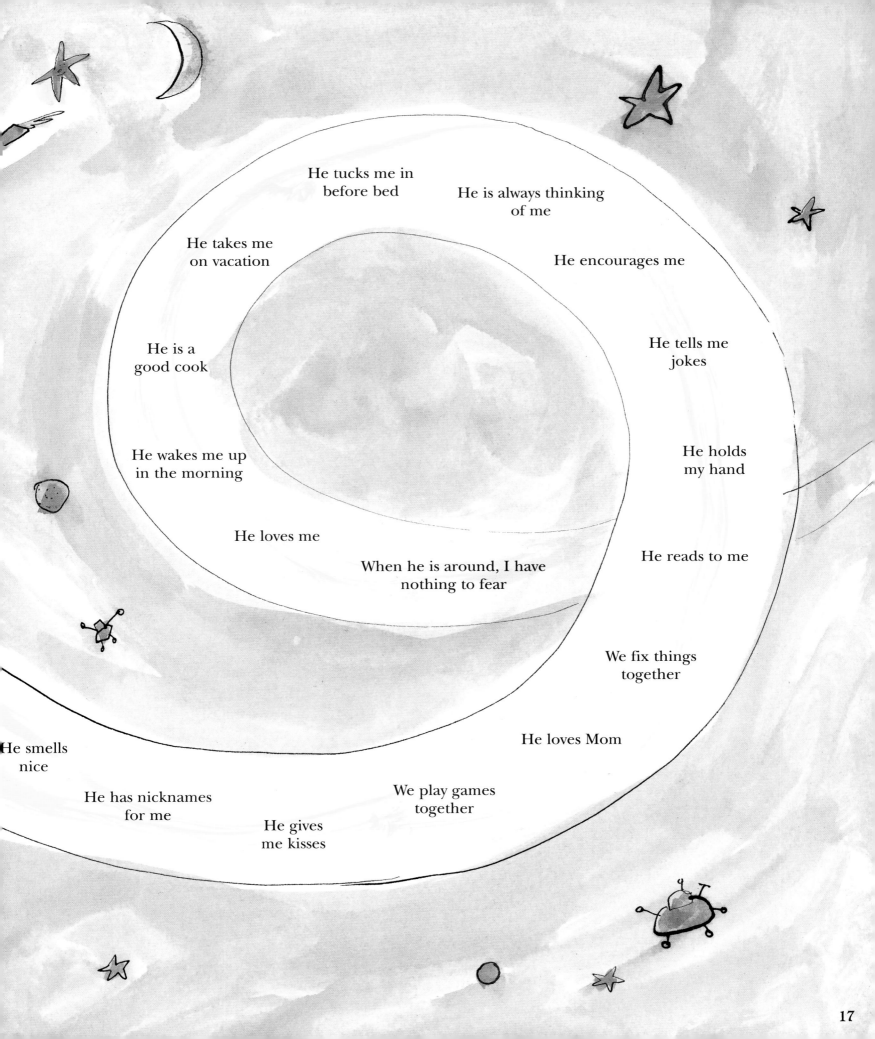

He tucks me in
before bed

He is always thinking
of me

He takes me
on vacation

He encourages me

He is a
good cook

He tells me
jokes

He wakes me up
in the morning

He holds
my hand

He loves me

When he is around, I have
nothing to fear

He reads to me

We fix things
together

He loves Mom

He smells
nice

He has nicknames
for me

We play games
together

He gives
me kisses

Life According to Dad

As you grow up, you will be able to share even more things with your dad—activities, tastes, conversations, and many, many laughs!

But right now is one of the best times to start learning about your father and about life as he knows it!

Snapshots of life with Dad

Here are two whole pages to paste or draw pictures of important moments you've shared with your dad. Don't forget to write in the places and dates!

Date:

Place:

Date:

Place:

Date:

Place:

Date:

Place:

When Parents Get Divorced . . .

Sometimes when parents get divorced, you see less of your dad. Try to continue to spend quality time with him—it is as important for him as it is for you!

The days without him can make you sad, and it is hard to understand some of the decisions your parents make. Sometimes you ask yourself: Was it my fault? Or will Dad forget about me and have a new life?

The only way to understand your dad's feelings about the separation is to talk to him. Never forget that your dad is still your dad. Even though he and your mom are apart, they will always try to give you the best that life has to offer.

Just the Two of Us

There are some things we can do only with our dads and other activities we get too big for.
There are some things we can learn only from our dads and other lessons we teach them.
There are some things we can say only to our dads and other questions only they can answer.
Do dads feel the same way?

A little notebook of special things you do only with Dad

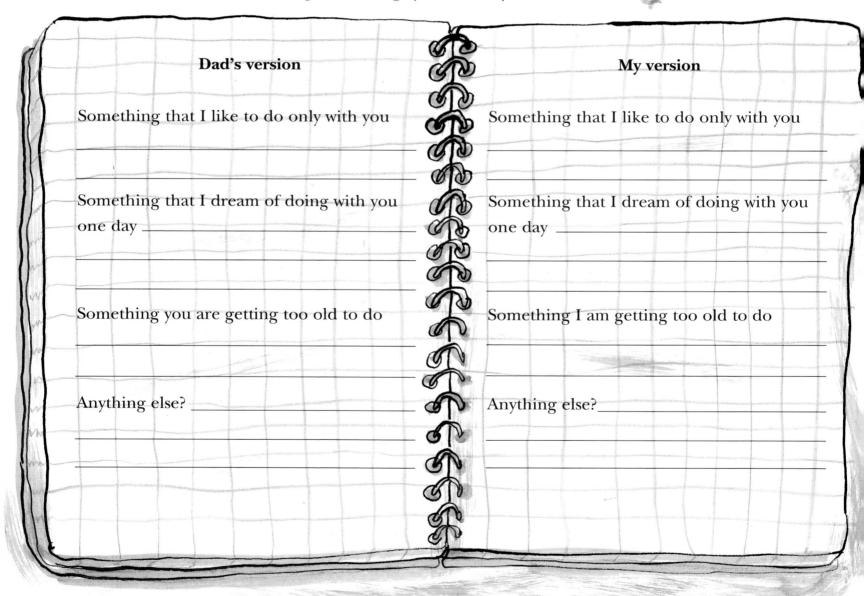

Dad's version	My version
Something that I like to do only with you	Something that I like to do only with you
Something that I dream of doing with you one day	Something that I dream of doing with you one day
Something you are getting too old to do	Something I am getting too old to do
Anything else?	Anything else?

Your dad does many things well, like building a fire, changing a tire, or fixing a leaking faucet. Ask him to write a little story about an activity he has learned to do perfectly.

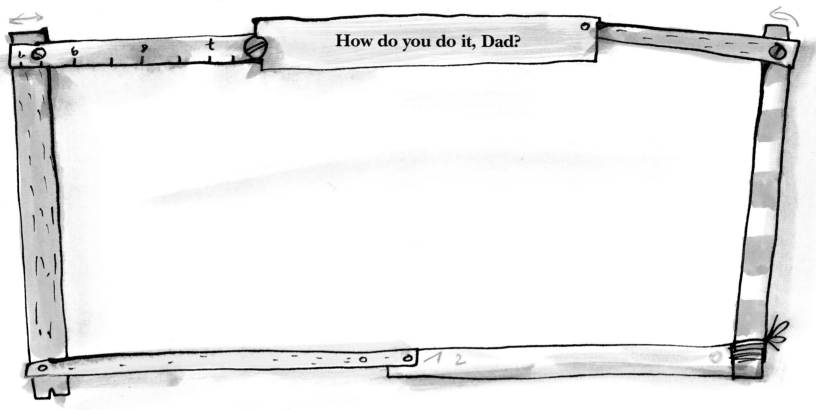

How do you do it, Dad?

Words of Wisdom

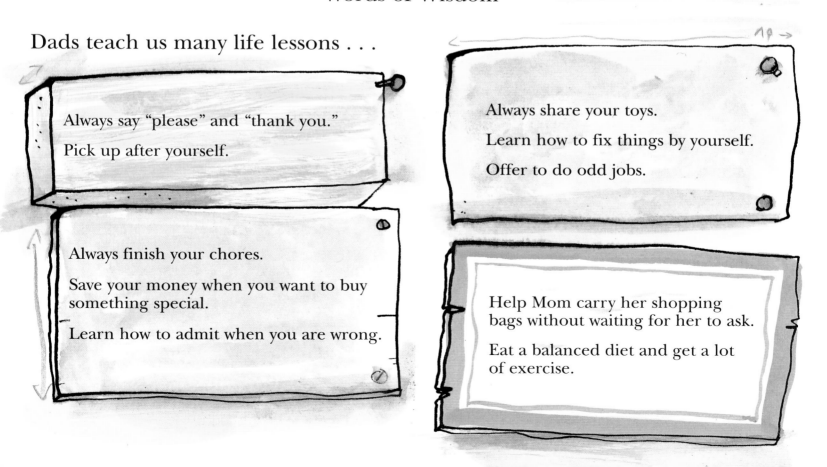

Dads teach us many life lessons . . .

Always say "please" and "thank you."

Pick up after yourself.

Always share your toys.

Learn how to fix things by yourself.

Offer to do odd jobs.

Always finish your chores.

Save your money when you want to buy something special.

Learn how to admit when you are wrong.

Help Mom carry her shopping bags without waiting for her to ask.

Eat a balanced diet and get a lot of exercise.

My Dad the Joker . . .

When it comes to goofing around,
dads are unbeatable.
It is time to take a moment
and do what everyone loves best—play!

Scary faces

Silly faces

Funny Face

*Take some pictures
of your dad
making funny faces.
Or if you can,
use one of those
photo booths
in the mall!*

The funniest story ever

*Make up a silly story
or draw a funny pic-
ture together*

. . . and the Adventurer

When you are with your dad—the sky is the limit!
Here are three little notebooks for you and your dad
to write down all of the amazing things you have
done or plan to do together.

Inventions

Together we have made

Adventures

Together we have explored

Discoveries

Together we have learned

Dad and His Job

To dads, work is very important.
He devotes a great amount of time and energy to his job.
Ask your dad to describe his career to you.
When did he start? Why did he choose it?
What are his days like?
Does his job make him happy?

In between jobs

Sometimes dads are without a job or looking
for a new one. This is often a difficult time, both
for parents and for kids. Ask your dad to tell you about
job-hunting—what is it like? Sometimes kids are
able to understand or even to help more
than their parents can imagine.

My Dad and His Life

Your dad is not only a dad. He also has friends, hobbies, ideas, and dreams.

Some dads often say: "I am juggling a lot right now!" This means he can feel a bit overwhelmed with all the things he wants and needs to do. Ask your dad to tell you about some of his outside interests.

In the juggling balls above, write or draw some of the things your dad likes to do when he is not at work or spending time with your family.

Newsflash

Most dads like reading the newspaper, watching TV, or listening to the radio. They love being up-to-date with what is going on. Pretend you are a journalist and interview your dad about how he sees the world around him.

Extra! Extra! Read all about Dad!

Ask your dad to tell you about a news story that influenced him.
Pay close attention and take many notes.
Write a report of your interview above and create your first news article!

Like a Lighthouse

Dads can teach you how to solve life's mysteries. They can help you make decisions and find your place in the world. Like a lighthouse, they are always there to guide your path and show you the way home.

Tell me, Dad!

What are your deepest wishes for your family? _____

_____

_____

What are the three personal qualities that you think are most important in someone?_____

_____

What are parents for? What is their biggest responsibility? _____

_____

_____

Do children have responsibilities, too?_____

_____

Do parents have secrets?_____

_____

Do you believe in God? _____

Do you practice a religion?_____

_____

Are you afraid of dying? And do you believe there is an afterlife?_____

_____

What does it mean to be a citizen? _____

_____

Why does everyone have to leave home someday?_____

_____

Look at me, Dad!

Take a good look at me today as I am.
Tell me what qualities or characteristics
you would most like for me to develop
as I grow older. What makes this so
important?

_____

_____

_____

_____

_____

_____

_____

Life Is a Journey

Sometimes it is hard to imagine what your parents were like before you were born. They had busy lives filled with comings and goings, experiences, and pastimes!

Your parents were on a special path before you came along, and with you, their journey continues. You, too, will have a unique journey of your very own.

My Dad's Family

Your father is also the son of his father and mother and the grandson of four grandparents. His history goes on for many generations into the past.

Ask your dad the names, dates, hometowns, and activities of his dad's parents (your grandparents) and his grandparents (your great-grandparents) and fill in this family pyramid. Don't forget about brothers and sisters, uncles and aunts, and others!

Once the pyramid is complete, you can see your dad's entire family history and half of your own!

My paternal grandfather

My paternal grandmother

Date:
Place:

Paste a photo of each of
your paternal grandparents.
Does your dad look more like one than the other?
And you? Do you resemble either of them?

Date:
Place:

In the orange boxes, write the names and birthdays of each member of your dad's family.

My dad

My paternal grandfather

My paternal grandmother

My uncles and aunts (Dad's brothers and sisters)

Our Family Name

It is common for a child to have the same last name as his or her father. If that is true for your family, ask your dad to write what he knows about your family name: What are its origins? Does the name have any special meaning? Does he know of other families with the same name?

_____

_____

_____

_____

My Dad as a Baby

Imagine your dad as a baby barely bigger than your arms! Do you know where and when he was born? Ask him to tell you the story of the day he was born or, even better, ask one of your paternal grandparents to write everything they remember about the day on the lines below!

Hey, Dad, did your parents have you baptized or did you have another kind of religious birth ceremony? If so, where and how?

_____

_____

_____

The names of my dad's godparents

_____

_____

A brief history of my dad's birth

_____

_____

_____

_____

_____

_____

_____

_____

_____

_____

Paste a baby picture of your dad in the frame above.
Look closely at the picture and mark with arrows all of the things
that are different for babies today: clothes, disposable diapers, toys, bottles, strollers…

My Dad as a Little Boy

Going to school, learning, playing, having fun, being scared, following the rules, making mistakes, being punished, getting sick . . . your dad did it all, too!

But how things have changed! In the next five pages uncover the life of your dad when he was younger.

Favorite photo of my dad as a child

Paste a photo of your dad as a kid—with his family, friends, or toys . . .
Don't forget to write the date the picture was taken!

Date:

Place:

Filmstrip of my dad as a kid

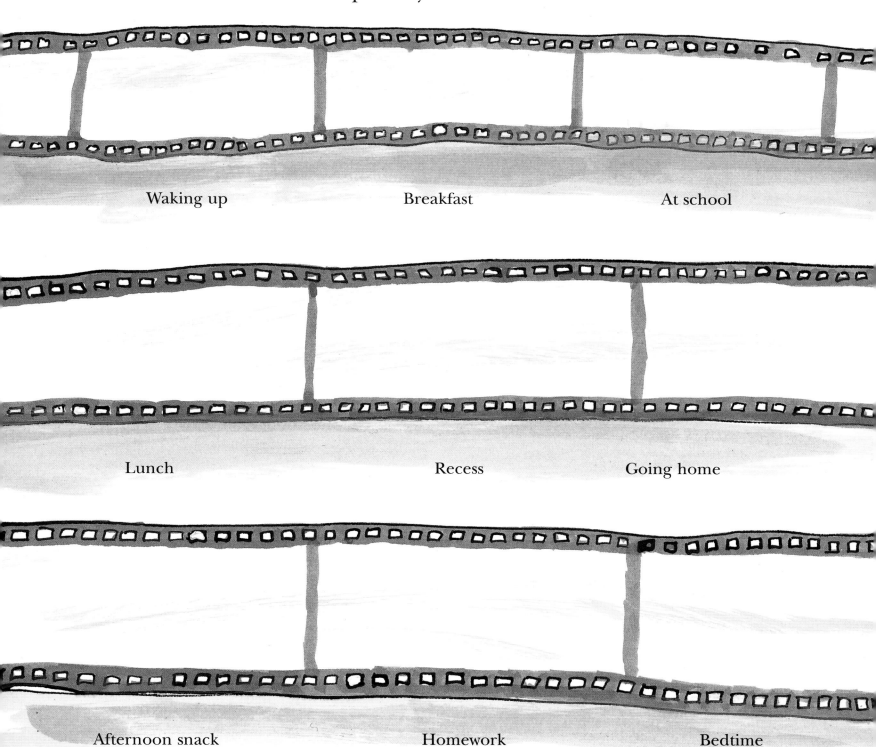

Waking up   Breakfast   At school

Lunch   Recess   Going home

Afternoon snack   Homework   Bedtime

There is no better way to get a sense of what being a kid was like for your dad
than seeing a movie about it. Create a filmstrip by drawing pictures, pasting photos,
and writing down as many details as possible about his day-to-day routine.
Remember to make note of the places, times, people, kinds of food, and more as you go.

Tell me, Dad!

The little things

Did you have a special object, favorite toy, or lucky charm? If so, what was it? _____
_____
_____

Did you go by a nickname? _____
_____

Did you have a pet? _____
_____

What was your bedroom like? _____
_____
_____

How did you dress? _____
_____

Did you ever get sick? _____
_____

*Hey, Dad,
did you ever throw a
tantrum?*
_____
_____
_____

*Hey, Dad,
which of your siblings did
you get along with best?*
_____
_____
_____
_____

Family life

Were your parents strict? If so, how?
_____
_____
_____

What did your dad always say to you? _____
_____

And your mom? _____
_____

Did you help with chores? _____
Did you see your grandparents often? _____
_____

Did they have any special names for you? _____
_____

Did you practice a religion as a family? _____
_____

What were your birthdays like? _____
_____

And holidays? _____
_____

Hey, Dad, did you ever wet the bed?

_____
_____
_____
_____

Hey, Dad, what was the best present you ever received?

_____
_____
_____

Hey, Dad, what was the dumbest thing you ever did? And what was your worst punishment?

_____
_____
_____
_____

Hey, Dad, what is your favorite childhood memory?

_____
_____
_____
_____

Hey, Dad, were you ever jealous of anyone? Why?

_____
_____
_____

Life with others

What was your favorite thing to do as a boy?

_____
_____

Who did you play with? _____
_____

What games did you play? _____
_____

Did you have a best friend? _____
_____

Did you ever get into a fight? _____
_____

Did you go on vacations?_____
_____
_____
_____

What sports or other activities were you into?

_____
_____

Don't forget about school, Dad!

What school did you go to? _____

_____

Did you get good grades? _____

_____

What was it like? _____

_____

Were the teachers strict? _____

Did you ever get punished? _____

Was it coed? _____

_____

What did you wear? _____

_____

What is your favorite memory of school?

_____

Did you eat at the cafeteria? _____

_____

What did you eat for lunch? _____

What is your least favorite memory of school?

What was your favorite subject? _____

_____

_____

_____

Did you ever get in trouble? _____

_____

What was your least favorite subject? _____

_____

If so, for what? _____

_____

Did you study alone? _____

_____

How did you get to school? _____

_____

Which subjects were easy and which were hard?

_____

_____

Anything else? _____

_____

_____

_____

My Dad as a Teenager

At around fourteen or fifteen years old, your dad became an adolescent. Little by little, he experienced his first facial hairs, his first boy-girl party, his first girlfriend, the horror of getting pimples, learning how to drive, and getting his first job.

These are some of everyone's most difficult years. Ask your dad to tell you more about what being a teenager is like!

Photo of my dad as a teen!

Date: Place:

My Dad as a Young Man

As a young man, your dad had to choose a path that would lead him to where he is today. The road to becoming an adult is different for everyone.

Some dads choose to have a family right away.

Some dads choose to travel the world before settling down.

Some dads choose a path that leads them to superstardom.

Some dads choose to study or work very hard at their careers before having a family.

And there is your dad who . . .

_____

_____

_____

_____

When Dad Met Mom

A mom and a dad are like two islands.
One day, a bridge is built between them—
a bridge of life, a bridge of love,
and a bridge built to last a lifetime—their child.

All parents have their own story
of how they came to meet
and later have a child.

*Ask each of your parents
to write on separate sheets
of paper about how they
met. Where? When? How
did they fall in love or
decide to get married?
In the boxes below, paste
each of their versions and
compare their stories.*

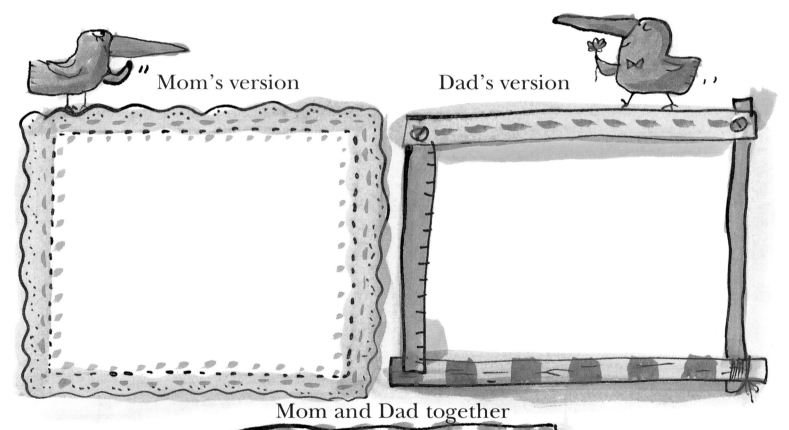

Mom's version

Dad's version

Mom and Dad together

*Look for a photo
with your dad of
the time when he
and your mom were
dating, or of their
wedding.*

Date:

Place:

Our Family

Y ou and your dad have a special love. Your dad also has enough love in his heart for everyone in your family! He shares it with your brothers and sisters, your mom, your grandparents, your aunts and uncles, and even your family pet!

Date:

Place:

Paste a photo above of your whole family.
Don't forget to include everyone's names and ages.

My Future as a Parent

What do you most wish for me in my adult life? _____
_____
_____
_____

In what ways would you like me to be like you? _____
_____
_____
_____

In what ways do you think I should be different?
_____
_____

Get out your crayons, Dad!

Ask your dad to draw what he imagines you will be like when you are old enough to be a parent.

45

Setting Sail

There will come a day when you are ready to
leave the boat that your dad has captained
and set off for uncharted waters
on your own ship.

However, no matter how young or old you are,
you will always love and need your dad
and he will always love and need you.

Here is an envelope
in which you and your dad can put
a special note for each other—
or a letter, a poem
a photo, or a drawing—
as a special present and memento
for you to exchange with each other
on the day you set sail.

Dad
and
Me

PAR AVION

Keepsake
Envelope

Contents

This book was created by

_____ and _____

on _____

Design by Sonia Chaghatzbanian
Production Manager: Jonathan Lopes
Translated by Rachelle Nashner

Library of Congress Control Number: 2004113782

Printed and bound in Belgium
10 9 8 7 6 5 4 3 2 1

Harry N. Abrams, Inc.
100 Fifth Avenue
New York, NY 10011
www.abramsbooks.com

Abrams is a subsidiary of

LA MARTINIÈRE
GROUPE

Dad, Papa, Father, Daddy,

Dear Dad, World's Greatest Dad,

Super Dad, Pop, Dadd

Dad, Papa, Father, Dad

Dear Dad, World's Greatest I

Super Dad, Pop, Dad

Dad, Papa, Father, D